IMAGES
of Scotland

Millport
& the
Cumbraes

A large group of holiday makers in the 1920s, posing on the beach in front of the Garrison at Millport.

IMAGES
of Scotland

Millport
& *the* Cumbraes

Martin Bellamy

TEMPUS

Crocodile Rock, Millport.

No trip to Millport is complete without a ride on the Famous Crocodile Rock.

First published 2003

Tempus Publishing Limited
The Mill, Brimscombe Port,
Stroud, Gloucestershire, GL5 2QG
www.tempus-publishing.com

British Library Cataloguing in Publication Data.
A catalogue record for this book is available from the British Library.

ISBN 0 7524 2790 3

Typesetting and origination by Tempus Publishing Limited
Printed in Great Britain by Midway Colour Print, Wiltshire

Contents

Acknowledgements

All the images in this book have come from the collections of the Museum of the Cumbraes in Millport and I am indebted to North Ayrshire Council for permission to reproduce them. Many people have helped, both directly and indirectly, to make this publication possible. Dorothy Thomson and the Friends of the Museum spent many years putting names to the faces and places in the photographs. Hamish Boyle spent a year at the museum meticulously identifying, cataloguing and filing the collections and most kindly read through the manuscript for me. I would also like to thank Susan and Finn for sleeping soundly while I worked on the manuscript.

All of the photographs are copyright of North Ayrshire Council Museums Service except for pp. 41 (bottom), 61 (top & bottom), 79 (top) and 91 (bottom), which are copyright Walter Kerr.

Sources

Much of the information used in this book has come from the archives of the museum. The following publications have also been most useful:

Campbell, J.R.D, *Millport and the Cumbraes: A history and guide* (Largs, 1975).
Chisholm, Alastair, *Millport Pier Album* (Largs, 1992).
Kerr, Walter, *Cumbrae Since the War* (Catrine, 2001).

Introduction

For most people the mention of Millport conjures up images of the heady days of the Clyde as a holiday paradise, with a trip 'doon the watter', a paddle on the sandy beaches and an ice cream from the Ritz Café. Millport is the only town on the island of Great Cumbrae, which is just a short ferry ride across from Largs. It became one of the most popular holiday resorts on the Clyde and with its pleasant climate, friendly atmosphere and wide range of attractions it was a firm favourite with the family audience. During the summer many families moved to the island to escape the noise and smoke of Glasgow. These seasonal residents, alongside the day trippers and holidaymakers, saw the population more than double during the summer months to make Millport a bustling vibrant little town.

The town began to develop as a holiday resort in the mid-nineteenth century but there is more to the island than just holidays. People have lived on the island since the Bronze Age or before. The early settlers were mainly farmers and fishermen and lived in a number of small hamlets dotted around the island. In the seventh century Saint Maura established a religious settlement on the island. Millport began to develop in the seventeenth century when the Clyde revenue, or customs, service stationed its cutter on the island. The development of a quay made access easier and further stimulated the growth of the town.

The island of Wee Cumbrae lies just to the south of its larger neighbour and has quite a different character. It is more rugged and isolated and has been home for only a small number of people over the years. Like its neighbour it had its own religious sect in the seventh century run by Saint Veya. It also had a castle that was used as a retreat by the Scottish kings.

The history of Millport and the Cumbraes has been rich and varied and is now once more moving into a different phase. Cheap foreign holidays have decimated Millport's holiday trade and the town now has an air of faded glory about it. However, it still has its own unique charm. It has never been overdeveloped and remains one of the best-preserved Victorian towns in Scotland. The island still remains very popular for day trips and you can still feel the buzz during the Glasgow Fair.

One

The Burgh of Millport

Cumbrae was, at first, only inhabited by a small number of fishermen and crofters. The turning point in the history of the island came around 1650 when the Clyde Revenue Service stationed their revenue cutter on the island and the crewmen began to settle in the Millport area.

The population began to expand when the harbour was built in 1797, seeing the population double to over a thousand by the 1840s. The oldest part of the town was naturally concentrated around the quayside but it soon expanded to the east and west. The population continued to grow as further extensions to the pier brought more prosperity and tourist trade. By the late nineteenth century the population had stabilised to around 1,500 permanent residents.

The Marquis of Bute and the Earl of Glasgow between them owned the whole of the island and they shared joint responsibility for its affairs. In 1864 Millport became a Police Burgh with an elected provost and town council. George Frederick Boyle, the sixth Earl of Glasgow, was the first Provost and served on the council for over twenty years. Under his leadership the town grew considerably and many new services were provided for the town. The council took great pride in their town and over the years provided it with a Town Hall, a hospital, a water supply and drainage system, a protective sea wall, a gasworks, a police service, a volunteer fire brigade and many other services.

Opposite: Provost John Taylor was elected as a Burgh Councillor in 1894 and was elected Provost in 1903. He is seen here seated in the Provost's chair wearing the burgh regalia.

The *Royal George* was one of the island's revenue cutters. It was commanded by Capt. James Crawford who was largely responsible for establishing Millport as a port when he had a new stone quay built. Many of the town's streets are named after men who served on the cutters, reflecting their importance to the development of the town.

On the back of the photograph is the following inscription: *Photographed A.D. 1881 by Joseph Horatio Ritchie of London from a watercolour drawing taken about A.D. 1780 which was long in the possession of Mrs. Daniel McKirdy, Millport, whose father, Charles Castello (or Castle) was Cutter's Steward and died in Cumbrae A.D. 1804.*

A view of Millport from the early 1860s showing the newly enlarged stone pier that was built to accommodate the ever-increasing size of ferries that were calling at the town. We can clearly see here how the development of the harbour stimulated the growth of Millport from a small village into quite a substantial town.

This is one of the oldest photographs of Millport, taken in the 1860s. The road along the seafront, Stuart Street, is still unmetalled and the sea wall has not yet been built. It shows the buildings that grew up around the quayside, including the Royal George Inn and the Cumbrae Hotel.

This photograph of Stuart Street taken around 1880 shows some of the businesses that developed in order to serve the growing town and its holiday trade. There is David Little the boot and shoemaker, the Temperance Hotel with its Coffee House, Millport Inn, a tobacconist, a fruiterer and William Templeton the flesher, or butcher.

Above: The Cumbrae Hotel was one of the first hotels to be opened in Millport. The original part of the building can be seen on the left-hand side where the hotel bar is. The later extension is on the right-hand side and incorporates a bazaar, a fruiterer and Macfarlane's butcher shop. In his guide to the town in 1886 William Lytteil states that the hotel was 'really a good house. Visitors to the island may put up here at moderate charges, and find their wants well attended to.'

Left: Somerville's Temperance Hotel was popular not only with visitors who had 'signed the pledge' but also with those who were simply seeking a quieter and more sober holiday. The hotel had a Coffee House attached to it rather than the more traditional hotel bar. In 1896 the local historian Dr McGown described the hotel as being 'a quiet comfortable establishment' where 'one will find charges moderate and hostesses obliging'.

Millport pier was originally owned by a private company, but in 1905 the Burgh Council purchased it for the greater benefit of the town. It was in need of a certain amount of restoration and the council took the opportunity of extending it to its present size. This enabled the largest excursion steamers to call at any state of the tide. Here we see the extension being built in the spring of 1906.

This view of Stuart Street from the pier around 1900 shows the seafront buildings in their final form. Apart from the shop fronts and the sea wall, the view is almost identical today.

The Millport burgh officials could be seen out in force for the celebrations for the coronation of King George V on 22 June 1911. *From left to right, front row:* Sergeant McRae; J.C. Sharpe; John Cunningham (baker and Burgh Councillor); Harry Wales (Burgh Councillor); Tom Clark (Provost); Robert Adams (Burgh Surveyor); Walter Kerr (coalman and Burgh Councillor); Mrs Mackay (wife of Cllr Mackay); Mr R. Crawford (farmer at Figgatoch and former Burgh Councillor).

The opening of the new gasometer in Millport in 1914. A gasworks was set up on the island in the 1840s by a private company. This was acquired by the council in 1896 who then set about improving it. *From left to right, front row:* John Dymock (Burgh Surveyor and gas manager); James McConnochie; ? MacLean; Robert Black; Alec Caldwell (Pier Master); Archie Cameron (Burgh Collector); Barr Morris (builder); Colin Millar (hairdresser); Adam Stewart (county district clerk). *Back row:* John McKenzie; George Duncan; Robert Copeland; Dr James Herbert Paul; George Hastie; John Ross; -?-.

Jimmy Ferguson was employed by the Burgh Council to make important announcements through the town. In a manuscript in the museum entitled 'Millport Memories' 'J.C.M.' recalls seeing him: *We often met up with Jimmy Ferguson, 'The Bellman', he was a character, not very tall and had a slight squint in one eye, but what a treat to hear his voice shout 'Notice, grand evening cruise tonight, leaving at 6.30pm, to Rothesay, fare adults 2/- 6, juniors 1/- 6', this with three rings of his bell at each stop.*

An isolation hospital was built on the island by the Burgh Council in 1901 and named in honour of Lady Margaret Crichton Stuart, Marquess of Bute. In 1929 it was taken over by Bute County Council. The Matron and Sister are seen here with guide officers at the opening of the new wing of the Lady Margaret Hospital on 16 March 1932. *From left to right, back row:* Jean Munro; Sister Kelty; Betty Kerr; Molly Cameron; Sister Dalziel; Grace Little. *Seated:* Mrs Ross (Matron); Marie McLachlan.

The two most important and imposing buildings on the island are the Garrison and the cathedral. The Garrison was originally built by Capt. Crawford of the cutter service. In 1819 it was purchased by George Boyle, fourth Earl of Glasgow, who rebuilt it as his own summer residence.

The Cathedral of the Isles was originally built as a private family chapel for George Frederick Boyle the sixth Earl of Glasgow, in 1851, to the design of the esteemed architect William Butterfield. It was later enlarged and handed over to the Episcopalian Church around 1870. It is said to be the smallest cathedral in Britain, if not Europe. Attached to the cathedral is a residential college where theologians can study using the extensive library. It is frequently used as a retreat for quiet contemplation in peaceful and pleasant surroundings.

George Frederick Boyle, sixth Earl of Glasgow, commissioned Butterfield to make certain additions to the Garrison while he was building the cathedral. He also had a boundary wall with two imposing gateways built around the grounds. After his death the Garrison was used for many years as the official residence of his widow, the Dowager Countess of Glasgow, who had the sunken gardens developed at the front of the house.

In 1948 the Garrison was leased to Millport Burgh Council as their headquarters. It served as the principal council office on the island until 1997 when it had to be vacated. In 2001 it accidentally caught fire and was completely gutted. The island's volunteer fire brigade are seen here the morning after the fire dowsing the flames. Despite its sad appearance there are great hopes for it to be renovated and turned into a community facility.

Millport steadily extended eastwards along the seafront. The area east of the Garrison is known as Newton and was built in the 1850s. The eastward extension continued round the corner into Kames Bay where the original boarding houses that form Kelburn Street were built. The one place where houses have been built on the seaward side of the shore road is the area known as Crosshouse just at the corner between Kames Bay and Newton.

Kameston was originally a separate village but by the 1860s it had been swallowed up by the town of Millport. Kames Bay is the most sheltered part of the town and was considered the most suitable residence for 'those afflicted with any disorder of the respiratory organs'. The bay was described in glowing terms by William Lytteil in 1886: *The sea in Kames Bay has the sheen of a mirror when the sun at eve strikes upon it and develops the soft gliding movements of a light and almost imperceptible swell, which rolls along in pearly iridescence and breaks upon the strand with a low, sweet, plaintive swish!*

West Bay was developed a little after Kames Bay and although slightly more exposed to the weather the views are spectacular. Many of the houses were designed as boarding houses rather than family homes, reflecting the growing importance of summer residents to the growth of the town. This view of West Bay looking toward the town dates from around 1890, before the road was built.

This view shows the full extent of the development of Millport along two and a half miles of seafront, from West Bay right round to the villas on Marine Parade at Kames Bay.

Two

Around the Island

The road around the shoreline of Great Cumbrae was completed in 1875 and, ever since, tourists have taken the opportunity to walk, cycle, drive or, in the early days, enjoy a horse and trap or charabanc trip around the island. There are numerous interesting sights to see along the coast, including strange geological formations, piers and beaches, not to mention places to take refreshment. Those who venture inland are rewarded with wonderful viewpoints and evidence of the island's prehistoric past.

Away from the town of Millport the island is relatively undeveloped and provides a number of different unspoiled natural habitats, from rocky foreshores to lush woodland. Among the native wildlife are black rabbits, hedgehogs, shrews, bats, butterflies, and a fine variety of wading and woodland birds. There is a rich and varied plant life on the island and it is particularly noted for its large variety of orchids.

Opposite: This 'Indian's Face' painted onto the cliff, peeping through the bushes, can be seen on the west of the island.

On the top of the island, at a height of 127m (417ft), is the Glaidstane viewpoint. On a clear day the view is one of the best on the Clyde, stretching from Ben Lomond right down to Wigtonshire, taking in the Argyll and Ayrshire coasts and the islands of Bute, Arran and the Ailsa Craig.

The Scottish National Water Sports Centre was opened in 1976, close to the ferry landing at Cumbrae Slip. It is ideally situated, as the waters here are relatively sheltered and safe for novices to learn in. The centre quickly developed a reputation as one of the best centres in the country for the teaching of sailing, canoeing and windsurfing.

In 1928 a mineral spring was discovered by Cllr John Freebairn a short way down the hill from the Glaidstane. The waters were analysed and found to contain iron 'in such quantities and in such a form as to be much desired by pharmacists and doctors'. The council seized the opportunity to develop the well and advertise its therapeutic effects. It was opened with all due ceremony by June Tripp, Lady Inverclyde on 14 May 1929. June Tripp was an actress and had starred alongside Ivor Novello in Alfred Hitchcock's *The Lodger* in 1926.

Right: Despite the initial excitement on its discovery, when 200 people queued to sample the water, the mineral well never achieved Cllr Freebairn's dream of turning Millport into a spa resort. The well did prove popular as a novelty and as a source of refreshment for those climbing to the top of the island, but gradually it fell into a state of disrepair. It remains as a monument to the island's grand ambitions.

Another mineral spring was to be found at Fintry Bay on the west coast of the island. This one was put to commercial use by 'Irish John' Kennedy the proprietor of the Fintry Bay Refreshment Bar. The café was celebrated in a song found in a collection called *Local Lyrics* written by T.B. in the museum's archives:

The old men love its coolness and the young men praise its fire,/ But its pure translucent sweetness universal joys inspire,/ But the maiden loves it most, for her whispering lover tries,/ To compare its glittering splendour to the sparkling of her eyes,/ Oh the Fintry water flavoured with the yellow fruit of Spain,/ Gains tribute from the traveller and praises from the swain,/ And may the streaming sunshine of each daily dawn/ See your happy bower still standing, Irish John, Irish John.

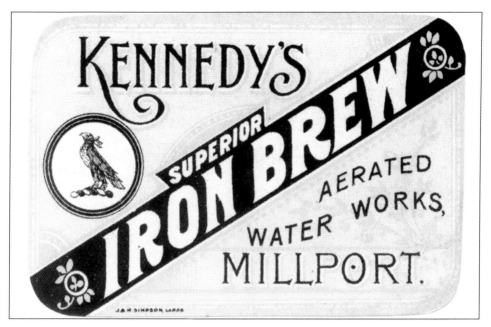

The Kennedy's set up their own 'carbonated water' works at Fintry Bay and produced all manner of drinks to delight their customers such as Ginger Ale, Sarsaparilla, Iron Brew, Cream Soda, and every kind of fizzy fruit drink you could wish for.

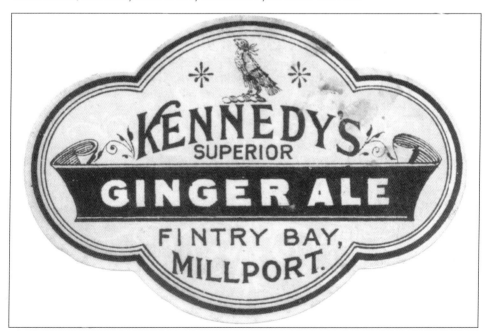

Opposite, below: Apart from the Refreshment Bar there were no amenities at Fintry Bay and it was favoured as a quieter beach, away from the throngs on Newton Sands or Kames Bay. It proved popular as the destination for a picnic, or a day out from the town of Millport, for the more energetic holidaymakers on the island.

On the east side of Kames Bay was to be found 'the Ark'. This was an old boat belonging to Dr John Murray that had been converted into a marine laboratory. Murray was a scientist aboard HMS *Challenger* which had sailed the world from 1872 to 1876 carrying out observations and surveys. He decided that Millport would be a suitable base to write up his findings and so, in 1885, he brought his floating laboratory to the island. This became a tourist attraction and for the charge of a penny visitors could come aboard and see the fine collection of marine specimens. The Ark was destroyed by a south-westerly gale in December 1900.

One of the scientists who worked aboard the Ark was Dr David Robertson, the 'Cumbrae Naturalist'. In the 1890s he decided that the Ark was too small and, with a group of his Glaswegian friends, raised the money to build a permanent research laboratory on dry land. Dr Robertson is seen here cutting the first sod for the Marine Biological Station on 7 August 1896. *From left to right:* Dr Rankin; -?-; James Allan (baker); -?-; G. McOre; Capt. Turbyue; P.M. Chalmers; Alastair Robertson (David's son); Dr David Robertson; John Taylor (joiner); Ex Provost Paterson; John McGraw; -?-.

The Marine Biological Station was opened in 1897 by Robertson's old friend Sir John Murray, but sadly Robertson had died before he could see the results of his efforts. The building included a laboratory, a library, an aquarium and a museum that was named in Robertson's honour. The laboratory carried out much valuable research over the years and in 1939 it was extended with the addition of a second, almost identical, building.

As the town of Millport developed it expanded considerably eastwards away form the existing pier. To serve this part of town it was decided that a new pier was required. Keppel Pier was built by Kennedy's of Partick and after several problems, including an accident with one of the cranes, it was opened to the public on 18 August 1888. As well as for serving passengers, the pier was also used by the Marine Biological Station and over the years various scientific recording devices were installed.

The *Marchioness of Breadalbane* landing at Keppel Pier. As well as providing access to the eastern part of Millport, Keppel Pier was also highly useful because in rough weather it was more accessible than Millport Pier. So much so that the timetables warned that in the event of unfavourable tide or weather conditions the steamers would call at Keppel instead.

The excursion steamer *Queen Mary II* approaching Keppel Pier. The Marine Biological Station can be seen in the foreground.

Lion Rock, Millport.

Above: All over the island there are strange rocky outcrops called dykes. These were formed by volcanic eruptions forcing their way through fissures in the sandstone surface. Gradually the sandstone was eroded leaving the harder volcanic rock protruding. One of the more celebrated is the Lion Rock, pictured here, so named because it bears a resemblance to a lion with its mane.

Right: Evidence of early settlement on Cumbrae can be seen in Craigielea Woods, which is also known as Standing Stones Plantation. This one standing stone is all that remains of what was once a circle of five.

Three
Holiday Isle

Millport first developed as a holiday town when steamships made it easy to travel down from Glasgow. By the 1850s a trip 'doon the watter' had become an annual highlight for many of the Clyde's workers. Millport always advertised itself as a peaceful and relaxed family resort with a friendly atmosphere. It did not have any of the garish attractions or seedy back streets of some of the other resorts, and the islanders did their best to make the holidaymakers welcome.

The busiest time for the town was during the Glasgow Fair in July when all the Glasgow factories and shipyards had their annual fortnight holiday. The population more than doubled, with families taking up residence in the many boarding houses along the shore, or lodging with local landladies. During a season there could be as many as a hundred thousand visitors passing through the pier turnstiles.

As well as the beaches and other natural attractions, there was also a whole host of entertainments for all ages, including restaurants and cafés, beach entertainers, donkey rides, ballroom dancing, cinema shows, sports of all descriptions and excursions by road or sea. Cheap foreign holidays have put an end to much of this trade but visitors still come to enjoy the beaches, cycle round the island, or see the illuminations.

Opposite: Children love nothing better than a trip to the seaside with their bucket and spade. This photograph shows two local children, Jess and Lee Howard, in a studio portrait by A.G. Wright of Cardiff Street, Millport. There were several photographers on the island who made their living from taking souvenir portraits of holidaymakers.

A holiday at Millport began with a trip on a steamer. There were regular connections throughout the summer form Largs, Fairlie and Wemyss Bay. Excursion steamers sailing from Gourock and Craigendoran also called at Millport on an almost daily basis. Here we see a scene from early in the twentieth century with a rather well-to-do crowd making its way off the pier.

The crowds throng from the *Glen Rosa* steamer which has just arrived at Millport Pier during the 1920s.

Above: Ginger McAllister ran a fleet of horse-drawn cabs on the island during the summer holiday season. Here we see the arrival of his horses and cabs off the steamer from the mainland. Seen here in this photograph is Alex Caldwell the Pier Master (third from right), Sandy Stewart (with the floury back), Jimmy Stewart, Willie Burnie, Ken McIntyre and Biddy the mare.

Right: Jack Shearer also operated a fleet of horse-drawn cabs but his pride and joy was his charabanc that offered trips around the island.

Sandcastle competitions were a regular feature of the summer programme of entertainments. They were held at all three of the island's sandy bays. This competition was held at Fintry Bay on 10 August 1923. The competition entries were often quite grand and huge crowds came to see what extravagant constructions had been made.

Another sandcastle competition during the 1920s, this time on Newton Sands, in front of the Garrison. Even up until the 1960s sandcastle competitions were held every fortnight throughout the summer.

Millport makes a special appeal to the children; in few other places is there such a delightful stretch of a nice sandy beach for their delectation. The beach is perfectly safe for them – here they can play all day long, getting the full benefit of the sun and the ozone. From the official guide to Millport of 1915. The message on this postcard reads: *Am staying here with Ellie for a day or two. Hope you are well. Love to you all from Ellie and I, M. June 21 1912.*

Beach Missions were a common sight and attracted large numbers of children to take part in a variety of entertainments such as chalk drawing and hymn singing. Here we see the United Free Church's mission on 20 July 1912.

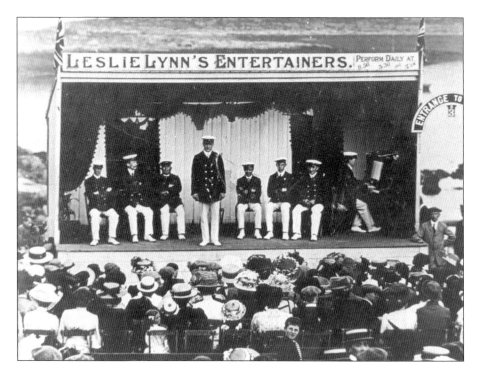

Leslie Lynn was a resident of Millport and, from around 1910 onwards, he brought a company of entertainers over from the mainland every summer. A stage was erected on the green at Crosshouse and for a modest fee of three pence, visitors were treated to a cabaret act of singing, dancing and comedy. A collection box was shaken in front of those hoping for a free show from behind the makeshift fences at the back.

This photograph shows just how popular Leslie Lynn's entertainments could be. The photograph is inscribed on the back: *To Miss Stewart from Mr Lynn, Millport 30/9/21*. Possibly Miss Stewart was one of the entertainers and this was her memento from Leslie Lynn at the end of the 1921 season.

The Albatross Quartette was another band of entertainers that put on a show for the summer crowds at Millport.

Most holidaymakers wanted to take home a souvenir of their visit and many businesses were set up to cater for this holiday trade. Cunningham's Picture Postcard Saloon not only sold postcards but also all sorts of knick-knacks and trinkets.

One of the ever-popular attractions for children is a ride on a pony or donkey along the beach. In 1900 the Burgh of Millport published a set of Bye Laws for the hiring of ponies and donkeys which stipulated that the animals had to be clean and free from infectious diseases. No one over the age of fifteen was allowed to ride on the donkeys and no one was allowed to ride the animals in a 'furious or reckless manner'. Bearing in mind the family nature of the business it comes as no surprise that it was also stated: 'owners and persons in charge of animals shall not use any obscene, quarrelsome or abusive language, gesture or behaviour, or be intoxicated, or conduct themselves in a disorderly manner'. Above is a pony on Newton Sands and below a donkey at Kames Bay.

Two boys playing on the crocodile rock. The rock was first painted around 1896 by a retired architect called Robert Brown. After rather too many drinks at lunchtime he saw the rock looking like a crocodile. The next day he came back sober with three pots of paint and painted the face in red, black and white. The rock has remained painted ever since.

The advent of the Box Brownie camera in 1900 enabled virtually anyone to take holiday snaps. The quality was not always great but at least the moment could be captured. Here we see one such example showing a family enjoying their holiday on the island in the 1930s.

Many a holiday romance was struck up during the Millport summers. Here we see a card posted from Glasgow in 1911 to Miss K. Stewart of Kelburne Street, Millport, probably as a memento from her holiday sweetheart. It reads: *Taken by the pal you mentioned on the pier. From Coo-o-o-ee Wee.*

The *Waverley* getting into the spirit of things for the Millport illuminations. The illuminations celebrated the end of the summer holidays and were a way of extending the season through to September. Lights were lit all along the seafront and there was a competition for the best illuminated display.

Today the holiday trade is just a shadow of its former self. However, many people still take a day trip to the island and it is almost obligatory to hire a bicycle and cycle around the island. (Photograph by Walter Kerr)

Three
Stormy Weather

Most people's memories of Millport will be of long, hot summers on the beach. However the weather is not always so kind to the island. Even in summer the weather can turn nasty quickly. In fact two boys were killed in an August storm on the island in 1904. Being exposed, out in the middle of the Clyde, the island can often bear the brunt of any storms, especially those coming in from the southwest.

A strong defence was necessary against the south-westerly winds and the Burgh Council spent considerable sums on maintaining and improving Millport's sea wall. The pier also had to be regularly repaired and it was virtually rebuilt on a number of occasions over the years after storms had wreaked their havoc.

The diary of David Crawford, a farmer at Figgatoch Farm during the early 1900s, gives testimony to the vagaries of Cumbrae weather. The entries showing 'fine day' are regularly interspersed with 'strong breeze blowing from the N. West' or 'dull day with heavy rain'. At one stage he was getting particularly fed up, noting simply, 'dull and wet all day and very disagreeable', a feeling that was probably all too common for those living on the west coast of Scotland.

Opposite: A windy day on top of the island at the Glaidstane viewpoint in the 1950s.

The storm of 26 November 1912 was one of the worst in the island's history, causing quite extensive damage to the seafront.

What price a seat on Spiers' windowsill having a chat during this? Rowat had a bad time as you may guess by the sea. The shop was washed out, windows, doors and everything.
Postcard from A.S. to J.H.W. Houston Esq., Custom House, Wuchon, China, dated 17 March 1913.

A combination of wild south-westerly winds and an exceptionally high tide saw Millport pier almost disappear underwater. It is seen here from a vantage point on Clyde Street.

The sea wall also saw considerable damage, as another postcard from A.S. to Mr Houston shows. *This beats November a year ago. It is a blessing the tide did not hold for another two hours on 26/11/12 or Millport front would have stood a bad chance of holding together.*

Not surprisingly the damage to the pier was considerable. This postcard, sent from A.S. halfway round the world to Mr Houston, simply states: *More of the damage caused on 16/11/12*.

P.S. *Caledonia* at Millport pier after a storm had played havoc with the pier's decking. The decking of the pier was not actually fixed down as the upsurge could cause even more damage. All the planks were numbered and they were simply replaced after a storm.

In order to minimise the risk of further possible damage to the town, the Burgh Council decided in 1929 that a new sea wall was to be constructed further out onto the beach. Here we can see the foundations being dug in front of the existing wall. As well as strengthening the town's defences against the sea it also meant that Stuart Street was made considerably wider.

The need for an improved sea wall can clearly be seen in this postcard.

Because of its exposed island location, Millport gets all the vagaries of the winter weather. Here we see the harbour and Stuart Street under a covering of snow in 1910. The pier staff however, were determined that the weather was not going to interfere with the working of the pier and they can be seen clearing away the snow with their shovels.

Snow of this depth is very uncommon on the island. Here we see Bute Terrace and the United Free Church snowed-in after a particularly heavy fall.

Garrison House looking splendid in the snow in 1910.

Five

Cumbrae Life and Characters

Life on the island had its own rhythm. During the summer there was all the hustle and bustle of the holiday trade with a huge influx of people. During the winter months life was much quieter and more relaxed for the islanders.

There has always been a real mix of society on the island. The Glasgow industrialists lived in the grand seaside villas with their servants, while the ordinary folk lived in the smaller houses and tenement flats. At one time the island even had its own cave dweller. However, despite all the social differences, there has always been a real community spirit on the island with numerous guilds, clubs and societies, as well as music and drama groups.

Like most small communities, Millport has had its fair share of colourful local characters, from lords and ladies right through to Irish navvies. Among the pillars of the community were ministers, doctors, politicians, businessmen and farmers.

Opposite: Granny Boyd having her tea at 24 Stuart Street, c.1900.

John Taylor and his family posing in their Sunday best. John Taylor was one of the well-to-do members of the community on the island. He ran one of the island's joinery firms and also served on the Burgh Council for many years, ending up as the Provost in 1903.

Taking a rest on the seafront in front of Shearer's dressmaking shop.

Copey Copeland was the island's paper 'boy' in the 1930s.

Left: Rab Dyer was an odd-job man and lived in a stable on Howard Street. He was known as 'The Nicker'.

Below: Crowds gather on the seafront to watch Provost Houston award the Royal Humane Society's medal to Eric Rafferty in 1928. (Centre of picture)

Andy Sullivan, or Fern Andy as he became known, was the island's recluse. He lived in a cave on the west of the island and sold little sprigs of fern to passers-by. He is celebrated in the song 'Andy the Fern Gatherer' found in T.B.'s collection of *Local Lyrics*:

> Though he sometimes seeks the village to see the works of men,
> He cannot long endure them but starts for home again,
> For the busy streets are dusty and the looks of all are cold,
> They think his joy is madness, his cheery word is bold,
> But he leaves them in their wisdom to think whate'er they list,
> And only wonders that so much of nature's wealth is missed,
> He lays his head upon her lap each night with calmness mild,
> And slumbers to her singing for he is nature's child.

Religious life has played an important role in fostering the town's community spirit and over the years there have been six different churches of varying denominations in Millport. Alexander Walker was the longest serving of the island's ministers. He was appointed as the minister of the Free Church in 1856 and during more than sixty years in post he became a well-known, if somewhat stern, face around the town. It has been said that during his ministry 'the Christian faith reached the zenith of its power in Cumbrae' and he invited many distinguished preachers and theologians to the island.

Revd James Frame was another of the island's long-serving ministers. He joined Millport's Presbyterian Church in 1884 and remained its minister until 1927. He is said to have probably been the finest of its ministers, 'whose warm evangelical appearance and constant parochial visitation endeared him to everyone of every denomination'. He is photographed here in 1920.

The Very Reverend Robert Oswald Patrick Taylor was the Provost, or senior priest, of the Cathedral of the Isles from 1919 to 1926.

Left: Granny Kennedy of the Fintry Bay Tearooms in 1947. Granny Kennedy was quite a character and was affectionately known as the Duchess of Fintry.

Below: Amateur dramatics have played an important part in the island's community life. Here we see the 'Co-optimists' from around 1910. *From left to right, back row:* John Freebairn (publican); James Hendry (tobacconist); William Templeton (butcher). *Middle row:* William Frame; Marie Grey; Nancy Templeton; Mary Paterson; Ina McDavid; Jean McKay (grocer); Donal Morrison (of Morrison's Omnibuses). *Front row:* Alex Hunter (boat hirer); Murdo McPherson; Martha McDavid; Jack Rowat (fruiterer).

Above: The car in this photograph, taken in 1922, was the first visitor's car on the island. The car was a Godfrey Nash and was owned by the Revd John A. Swan of the Ramshorn Kirk in Glasgow. The Revd Swan is pictured at the wheel. The small boy in the photograph is Donald Swan, who later became the artist of the Cumbrae Pottery, and the baby is Ian Swan who became the Mayor of Clarenville, Newfoundland, Canada.

Right: Mrs Watt tending her garden at her house 'Cairndhu' in West Bay, Millport.

Above: An impressive procession for the RNLI annual lifeboat day in 1951.

Left: Mrs J. Millar and Mrs M. Kerr enjoying the kind of weather that is all too familiar to Millport residents. Mrs Millar was the President of the Millport branch of the Ladies Lifeboat Guild and the two ladies are seen here collecting on Lifeboat Day, 25 September 1965.

The Old Peoples Welfare Association on the island enjoying a 'mannequin parade' by Bute Tweeds in 1960. (Photograph by Walter Kerr)

The Christmas party of the Millport branch of the Scottish Women's Rural Institute at the Town Hall in 1967. *From left to right, seated*: Mrs Steele; Mrs D. McFarlane; -?-; -?-; -?-; -?-; Miss Douglas; Mrs Templeton; Mrs Dick; Mrs C. Morrison. *Dancing*: Miss B. Dick; Mrs A. Rae; Miss M. Smart; -?-. (Photograph by Walter Kerr)

Six

School Days

The first schools on the island were set up either as small private concerns, or else they were run by the churches. There were perhaps eight separate schools operating by the 1870s. As a result of the 1872 Education Act a school board was set up and all these various different schools came under its jurisdiction. A new school was built in 1876 and named Cumbrae Public School. Virtually all the children on the island, approximately 200 to begin with, went to this new school. The staff consisted of just a headmaster and a handful of teachers.

Cumbrae Public School taught pupils up to the school leaving age of fourteen. Any pupils wishing to continue their education usually went off to Rothesay where they had to stay during the week. In the late 1970s it was decided that the island's children would travel to the newly improved Largs Academy for their secondary education and the island school was re-named Cumbrae Primary School.

The school has always had a vibrant social life with various different sports, drama and musical activities. The school choir was particularly well regarded.

Opposite: Boys from Cumbrae Public School. *From left to right, back row:* John Weir; Walter Kerr; Willie Forrest. *Front row:* Malcolm McInnes; John Campbell.

Cumbrae Public School catered for around 200 pupils when it was first opened in 1876. The school has seen many alterations and extensions over the years as educational needs have become ever more sophisticated.

William Lowe's class. The exact date of this photograph is not known but Mr Lowe was appointed on 2 November 1895 and left on 27 January 1901. *Boys from left to right, back row:* Archie McConnochie; ? Stewart; ? Reid; Neil Little; -?-; ? Graham. *Front row:* ? Kerr; ? Ferguson; -?-; Colin McInnes; -?-.

Miss McDougall's class at Cumbrae Public School in 1904. There was no school uniform at this time but the boys have all been turned out in their best clothes for the picture. Most of them are wearing starched collars but the mother of the boy in the lace collar in the front row must have been determined to make an impression, even if the boy doesn't look entirely happy about wearing it himself.

In one of the sandcastle competitions on the beach in 1908 a group of boys decided to make a model of Cumbrae Public School.

Cumbrae school staff in 1909. *From left to right, back row:* J. Dickie; Mary Young; Sergeant Blues. *Front row:* Miss McDougall; Robert Paterson (Headmaster); Miss Morrison.

A gym class in the grounds of the school, c.1900.

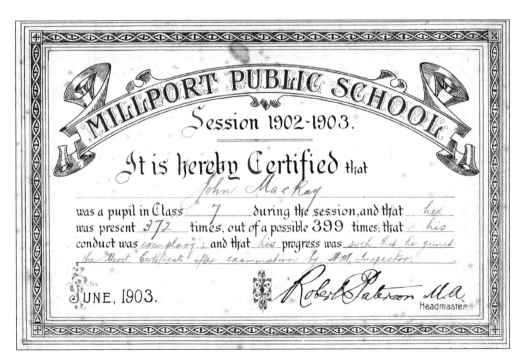

School certificate awarded to John MacKay in 1903.

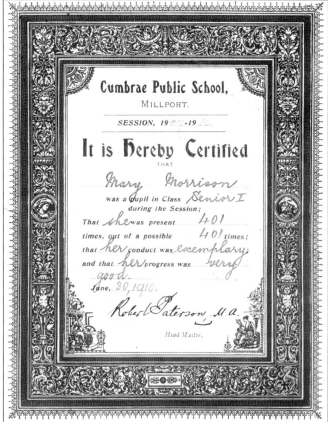

Above: The girls' class at Cumbrae Public School, c.1904.

Left: Mary Morrison's certificate from 1910. Mary was obviously a model pupil, not missing a single session throughout the term and having exemplary conduct.

Miss McDougall's class at Cumbrae Public School in 1913. *From left to right, back row:* Chrissie McIntyre; Agnes Connel; Nan Risk;-?-; Mollie Cameron; Nan Cunninghame; Annie Muir; Jessie Hill. *Third row:* Eadie Ferguson; -?-; Nancy Blair; Agnes Frame; Jean Shields; Margaret McLaughlan; Mollie McFie; Margaret Kerr; ? MacMillan; ? Wotherspoon; Marion Mauchline; Jessie Graham; ? Weir. *Second row:* Matthew Dickie; Tom Stewart; Andrew Mathewson; Colin Cassels; Alex Robertson; -?-; -?-; Jackie Cunninghame;-?-; ? Donald; Ella Graham. *Front row:* Malcolm Munro; Bobby Graham; -?-; -?-; -?-; Alex Stewart; -?-; -?-; Donnie Kerr; James Crawford; John Kennedy.

Mrs Crichton's class, the advanced division, in 1939. *From left to right, back row:* ? Kennedy; Wilson McKinnon; Nicol Thompson; George Clark; Bill Wilson; Mrs Crichton; W. Counsell; Jim Finlayson; G. Smart; Edward Morgan; Robert Hill. *Front Row:* Effie Osborne; Isabel McDermid; ? McLean; Sheila Watt; Frances Kelly; Jean Hill; ? Murray; Rita Tempini; Mamie Frame. *On the floor:* -?-; Eleanor Henderson.

Miss Willis with her primary two and three class enjoying a visit to Newton Sands in the 1950s. *From left to right, back row:* Edith York; -?-; -?-; -?-; Janice Blair; Mary Elliott; Murray Dalrymple; Margaret Ann Greaves; Hazel Beaddie; Madeline Gormon; Arthur Miller; Stuart Davidson. *Middle row:* -?-; Patricia Shields; Moira Stewart; Grace Little; Margaret Morgan; Freda Morgan; Susie Keaney; Margaret Boll. *Front row:* -?-; Willis Deans; -?-; -?-; -?-; -?-; -?-.

The Cumbrae School Choir on their way to the Arran Festival in 1957. Miss Kadenhead, the music teacher, is on the left and Mrs Kerr the accompanist, is on the right. *Pupils from left to right, back row:* Joan Cuthbertson; Hazel Beaddie; D. Hood; Mary Elliott; Patricia Kerr; Pat McKnight; Patricia Clark; Katherine Cuthbertson; Sheila Stewart. *Front row:* R. Logan; Mario de Angelis; A. Meechan; Graham Clark, M. Seaton; John Lumsden; Michael Meechan; Vera Hill; Christine Stevenson; Moira Fraser; Anne Welsh; Maureen McCracken; Rae Pollock; Edith York; Grace Little.

Right: Mrs Macrae with Katie Barbour and Elaine Hanlon on their first day of school on 23 August 1967. This was the first time that Cumbrae School had catered for special needs education.

Below: Inside a classroom at Cumbrae Primary in 1976.

Robert Hunter, Millport.

Seven

Working Life

Farming was probably the first occupation to be carried out on the island. It is said that Great Cumbrae is like a chunk of mainland Ayrshire in terms of its landscape and it has certainly proved similarly productive in terms of its agriculture. The farms tended to be a mix of arable and livestock with sheep and cattle grazing alongside crops of oats and barley. Potatoes were one of the island's most important crops. There was even a pier called the Tattie Pier, where the potatoes were loaded onto ships for the mainland.

Being an island it was inevitable that fishing and shipping were to play a large part in the island's economy and many islanders were employed at sea in various forms. The famous Clyde puffers were regular visitors to the island, bringing in supplies such as coal and timber and taking away the goods and foods that were made on the island. The Clyde pleasure steamers also provided a source of maritime work for the islanders.

Even before Millport developed into a major town there was a quarry supplying building stone on the island. As the town grew there was increased demand for the building trades and we find many joiners, slaters and builders setting up business on the island. As the town developed into a holiday resort a great deal of work was also to be found in servicing the holiday trade, from hotels and bars, to coach operators and funfairs. This work was naturally seasonal and many people moved to the island to find work over the summer months.

Opposite: Fine morning, but by 9 o'clock a slight shower of rain fell which put a stop to the inputting. Got in half a dozen carts, three to the barn and three to a stack. Went round with the first cart of potatoes for this season. Cutting all afternoon at the corn. Got in two stacks and two carts. Started to rain again about six o'clock. Entry from 14 October 1903 in the diary of David Crawford, farmer at Figgatoch Farm, Isle of Cumbrae. A copy of the diary is held in the museum.

Feeding ducks at Mid Kirkton Farm. Many of the island's farmers kept ducks and chickens as a means of supplementing their income as well as supplying their own table.

The farmer of Lower Kirkton Farm and his daughters in their Sunday best take time out to feed the chickens.

Right: The manufacture of textiles was a significant cottage industry on the island. Knitting, spinning and weaving were common occupations. Some islanders even turned their hand to lace making and the manufacture of 'Ayrshire Whitework' embroidered christening gowns.

Below: Miss McInnes ran a dressmaking business on the island. She is seen here with her staff of young girls. *From left to right:* Mina Stewart; Miss McInnes; Miss Rae; Jean McEwan; Mary Hunter.

Oil was needed on the island to lubricate the farm machinery and to oil the leather harnesses and so on. Rather than purchasing expensive whale oil from the mainland, some enterprising islanders went out shooting porpoises. John Shearer and his three sons Alec, Hugh and Willie are seen here in 1897 with their catch on the Eileans in Millport bay. They would light a fire on the Eileans and smelt down the livers to get a rich supply of oil.

Here we see the island blacksmith Robert Morris and Robert Taylor with another fine catch of porpoises.

The crew of the Clyde steamer *Marchioness of Breadalbane* included many Cumbrae men. *From left to right, back row:* -?-; -?-; -?-; -?-; Willie Lafferty; Duncan Sinclair; -?-; -?-; -?-. *Front row:* -?-; Archie McPhail; -?-; ? Waterson (Chief Engineer); Capt. Dan McInnes; ? McIntyre (Purser); -?-; Wee Geordie Ferguson (Mate); -?-.

Millport pier was always a scene of great activity with all the comings and goings of cargoes and visitors. The Pier Master Alec Caldwell is seen here with his men proudly posing in front of a cargo of foodstuffs that has just been unloaded onto the pier. *From left to right:* W. Stirrit; -?-; -?-; B. Douglas; -?-; A. Carstairs; D. McLachlan; Alec Caldwell; W. Kerr; ? Stewart.

Above: Unloading a cargo of coal from the *Mary Kerr* around 1900. It was a long and laborious task to unload a cargo such as this. The ship's yardarm was used as a crane but it could only lift one small bucket at a time from the hold onto the waiting cart.

Left: A couple of old salts, no doubt from a ship landed at Millport pier, enjoying a rest on the seafront beside the war memorial.

Right: About fifty years on, the scene was still much the same. The steam puffer *Saxon* now carried the coal to the island but it was still unloaded bucket by bucket using the ship's own derrick. Mind you, the task of unloading the coal must have been much easier with a steam-powered winch. (Photograph by Walter Kerr)

Below: A group of tourists pose with the workmen unloading coal from a puffer, most likely *Saxon*, landed on the shore somewhere on the island.

Many of the islanders worked for Millport Burgh Council. Here we see a group of workers at Kames Bay posing in front of the burgh's very own traction engine that was purchased in 1914.

Council workmen laying the foundations of the new sea wall at Stuart Street in 1930.

By the 1880s Garrison House was in need of serious structural renovation. Its owner George Frederick Boyle, sixth Earl of Glasgow, hired a sizable group of stonemasons to carry out the work. They are seen here in 1887.

John Taylor owned one of the island's joinery firms. He is seen here with his workforce in 1897. *From left to right:* Douglas Robertson; Archibald Caldwell; John Taylor; Tom Houston; Bob Taylor.

Many people were employed in the shops that catered for the needs of the holidaymakers on the island. McNicol's Confectioners, established in 1886, was one of the favourite sweetie and ice cream shops along the seafront.

The post office was one of the most important lifelines on the island, keeping the locals in touch with the wider world and sending off the thousands of holidaymakers' postcards. Here we see the staff of 1908 outside the post office on Stuart Street. *From left to right:* Willie Bartholomew; Neilson Campbell; Jackie Little; Polly Rowatt; Miss Cunninghame; James Cunninghame; Kate Murdoch; Malcolm McInnes; James Ferguson (bellman); William Stirrit; -?-.

Many youngsters found work in the summer months working for the holiday trade. Here we see a young boy with his pony and trap at Keppel Pier around 1900. In his manuscript held in the museum 'J.C.M.' recalls working during his holidays: *My next adventure was to attach myself to Mr McLachlan who ran a nursery at the top of Cardiff Street. He had a pony and cart and together we moved around calling 'vegetables, vegetables', it was my duty to carry the goods to the housewives on our travels.*

A. Houston was the local fishmonger and poulterer. He also served on the Burgh Council from 1918 to 1930, ending up as Provost in 1927. The island had its own fleet of fishing boats and while much of their catch would be landed at the markets on the Ayrshire coast some of the fish would make it back to the island for Mr Houston's shop and for the hotels, cafés and restaurants serving the ever-popular fish teas.

Eight

Sporting Life

Sport has played an important part in the community life of Millport. There are numerous sporting clubs catering for a range of physical exertions from golf and bowls to football and yachting. These clubs provided a focus for the entertainment and recreation of the islanders all year round. Most sports were naturally played during the summer but curling and an annual bowling match were played in winter.

The sporting facilities were one of the great selling points for Millport as a holiday resort. Many of the sporting events were for spectators only, such as some of the football games and bowling championships, but competitions between the holidaymakers and the residents were also a common feature. These competitions were one of the reasons why Millport was considered such a friendly resort.

During the summer months a full-time sports organiser was employed on the island to arrange all the events and competitions. Among the sporting entertainments on offer were waterskiing, crazy golf, the tennis socials and open-air table tennis, and trampolining.

Opposite: Larking about on the golf course at Millport.

A view of the first tee of Millport Golf Club around 1907. The hill was known as Mount Pisgah, an Old Testament reference to Moses seeing the Promised Land. The original members obviously viewed their little golf club with high esteem! The official holiday guides were equally enthusiastic claiming that the course had 'the most breathtaking views in the world and air like champagne'.

A visitors versus residents tournament on 23 August 1911. Millport Golf Club was actually established in Glasgow in 1888 and its membership has always been made up of a mixture of Millport residents and 'overseas' members. Tournaments between the two groups of members were common. Holidaymakers could also take out temporary membership for their time on the island.

GOLF MATCH AT MILLPORT, JULY 23, 1913.
J. H. TAYLOR AND EDWARD RAY V. JAS. BRAID AND GEO. DUNCAN.

During the Glasgow Fair of 1913, Millport Golf Club played host to an international match featuring the cream of English and Scottish golfers. The two Englishmen J.H. Taylor and Ted Ray had won a total of six open championship titles between them and the Scots pair of James Braid and George Duncan could count five titles. These were perhaps the most famous golfers of their day and it was a real coup for Millport to host such a match. Over a thousand spectators attended the event and they were treated to 'one of the finest exhibitions of professional golf' and saw George Duncan smash the course record by six shots. The Scots won in the morning's play and the English fought back in the afternoon to leave the match tied.

TAYLOR   RAY   DUNCAN BRAID
INTERNATIONAL GOLF MATCH AT MILLPORT

Women were a common feature on the Millport golf course. The first ladies' competition was held as early as 1891.

OPENING OF MILLPORT BOWLING GREEN 16/5/14   G KEPPIE PHOTO.

Millport has had a bowling club since 1871. Here we see the opening of the greens for the summer season on 16 May 1914. The 'x' on the left-hand side apparently marks the location of Ina and Jean.

The opening of the greens on 18 May 1929. Millport's three greens were considered among the finest in the west of Scotland and the annual pairs competition during the Glasgow Fair used to attract hundreds of visitors from all over the country.

There is a Millport tradition of playing an annual bowling match on the 2 January, weather permitting. Here we see a hardy bunch well wrapped up against the cold ready to start the match in 1939.

The Millport junior football team at the West Bay playing fields in 1923. *From left to right, back row:* -?-; C. Cassels; D. McLachlan; J. Reid; J. Stewart; -?-. *Front row:* W. Gray; ? Kerr; Mr Lindsay; R. Wright; ? Kerr. *Goalie:* J. McDavid.

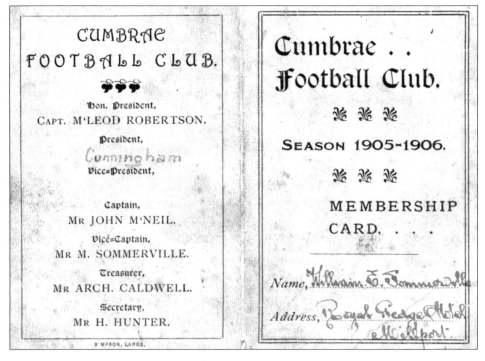

William Somerville's membership card for the Cumbrae Football Club's 1905-1906 season. Annual membership cost two shillings. Among the rules of the club it was stated that 'no profane language shall be allowed on the field'.

The senior football team at West Bay playing fields on 31 May 1922.

The Millport ladies football team c. 1970. *From left to right, back row:* Kathleen Atkinson; Isobel Anderson; Christina McIntyre; Rowena McPherson; Anne Lawson; Ella Demarco. *Front row:* Hazel Beaddie; Sheila Morris; Margaret Wright; Heather Warwick. (Photograph by Walter Kerr)

The Millport tug of war team in the early 1900s. *From left to right:* A. Stewart; -?-; G. Finnie; A. Houston; D. Crawford. *Seated:* Robert Adam (the Burgh Surveyor).

The opening of Millport's tennis courts in the 1920s. These courts were situated near to Kames Bay but were abandoned in favour of three new courts that opened in 1950 at the side of Garrison House.

A curling match on Cumbrae's curling pond at the top of the island. Curling was a popular sport on the island but was obviously dependent on a good freeze. Weather permitting, the teams from Millport and Rothesay would compete for the Dumfries Cup. The building at the edge of the pond was the clubhouse where all the stones were kept.

Another curling match on the island. It is interesting to note the different footwear of the players. Some have skates, others have ordinary shoes, while some have sacking wrapped around their feet. This not only prevented the ice being cut up by 'tackety' boots but also no doubt helped to insulate the wearer's feet from the cold.

Yachting on the Clyde was extremely popular and from the 1890s through to the 1930s massive yachts such as these could be seen racing each other. The Clyde Fortnight, during the first two weeks of July, saw thousands of visitors flock to the coast to witness these fiercely contested races.

Above: Sailing on a much smaller scale became possible in Millport when the Kames Bay boating pond was built. This provided a safe area for children to sail their model yachts. Here we see Mrs Clark performing the opening ceremony on 13 June 1925.

Right: A portrait of two island children, Eleanor and Jim Grant. No doubt Jim would have enjoyed trying out his model yacht on the boating pond.

Opposite below: The big yacht races were strictly a spectator sport for most people but it was possible to hire small yachts on the island. There is enough shelter for holidaymakers to enjoy pottering about in the bays but also enough excitement in open waters to test the more experienced sailors. For the serious yachtsmen there was an annual Cumbrae regatta held during August.

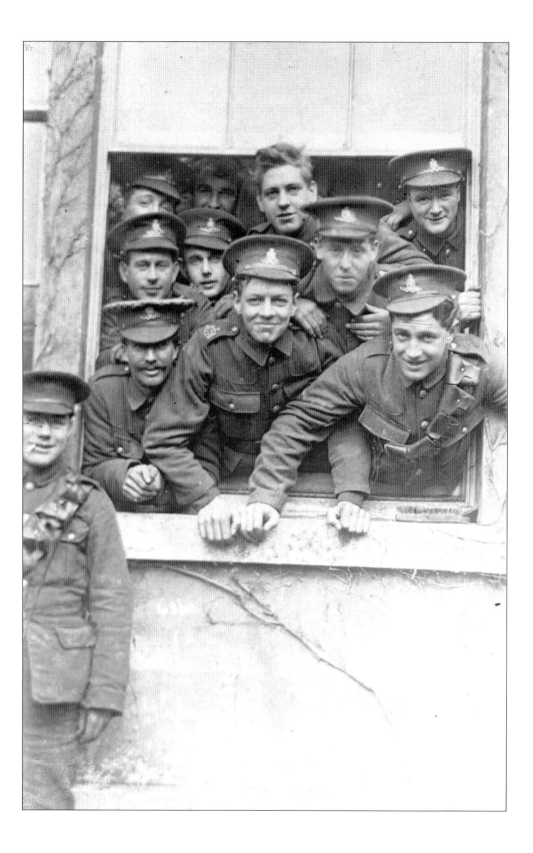

Nine

An Island Goes to War

The island has had a long involvement in military affairs, with a volunteer militia being recruited as early as 1797 as a defence against Napoleon. A firing range was laid out on the west of the island where the volunteers could practice their shooting skills.

Like most small communities, Millport lost a significant proportion of its men to the two world wars. The advent of the First World War saw large numbers of islanders enlist into the Bute Mountain Battery, a division of the Royal Garrison Artillery. They were initially sent to a training camp near Bedford before going off to fight on the Western Front in April 1915. During the Second World War most island volunteers again enlisted with the Royal Artillery although with so many islanders employed in the maritime trades some men preferred to go into the navy.

Cumbrae itself played an important role during the war. A defensive boom was erected across the Clyde from Cumbrae to the mainland, restricting any possible access by enemy submarines. On the north west of the island a submarine listening station was built and because of the secrecy surrounding its operations it was nicknamed 'Hush-hush' by the locals. Several hundred children were evacuated to the island and were put up as best they could by the local inhabitants. The evacuees saw the school roll more than double to around 650 children. The relative safety of the island also saw the Garrison being converted into a military hospital and many of Millport's women enlisted as volunteer nurses.

Opposite: A party of Millport men from the 4th Highland (Mountain) Brigade R.G.A. (Bute Mountain Battery) pose for the camera during their training before going off to fight in the First World War. Among the men are Duncan Weir; Alick Wright; Ike Morrison; Jimmy Finnie; Matt Wallace; Hugh Kennedy and John McDavid.

Making an impressive sight as they march down Stuart Street are the 4th Highland (Mountain) Brigade at the start of the First World War. The parade was no doubt designed to help raise more recruits from the island.

Opposite, below: Even the island's horses went off to war. Volunteers from the Bute Mountain Battery took their horses with them. Among the men are Sandy Stewart, Willie Burnie, George Finnie, James Crawford, John Kennedy and Jack Shearer. Also shown is Alex who wrote this postcard to Miss M. Hannah of Carlton House, Millport:

This is a PC of us leaving the pier on the Sunday at Millport and I hope you will manage to make me out. This is where I waved with the white handkerchief, the only one that was waving, Alex, Bedford, 22 August 1914.

Crowds gather to see off Millport's first volunteers for the war in August 1914.

A group of soldiers on horseback. The postmark is Bedford, where the regiment was posted for training before going off to the front.

To Miss M Hannah, 33 Holmhead Street, Cathcart.
Just a PC to let you see how we spent the Sunday here after church, of course there is not much difference to us here as Sunday and Saturday are much alike, Alex.

A postcard from gunner Jack Shearer, Bute Mountain Battery, Home Defence, Edinburgh, to Miss Polly Ewing, Baraar, Millport, 1914.

Dear Polly, just a few lines to let you know how we are getting on. We arrived on Thursday and have been getting drilled ever since to some tune. Hoping this finds you well and leaves me in the same. I remain truly yours ever, J. Shearer.

Matt Lawson on horseback at Scotton Camp in Catterick in 1917.

A group of soldiers from the Bute Mountain Battery in a field on Bute Terrace, Millport in 1914.
  To Miss M. Hannah, Carlton House, Millport.
Dear Martha, I don't know whether I sent you one of this or not. It was taken at the field opposite the hall before we left. Hoping you are keeping better, yours ever, Alex.

Soldiers standing beside a crashed plane. It is not clear whether this incident happened on the island or whether the photograph was brought back from elsewhere as a souvenir.

A light-hearted moment during training for the Bute Mountain Battery at Barry Camp in Bedford.

Few postcards survive after the initial training camp ones, no doubt due to the work of the censors. In total, forty-two Millport men were killed during the First World War. A war memorial was erected to their memory on the front at Stuart Street and was unveiled on 15 October 1922.

Despite the horrors of the war, the victory was celebrated in all manner of ways. Here we see an open-decked carriage from Millport that has been christened *The Victory* in honour of the 'Great War'.

CUMBRAE WAR MEMORIAL 1922

Left: The design for the war memorial. The inscription reads 'Valiant in Strife – Victors in Death'. After the Second World War the names of a further nineteen Millport men were added to the rear of the monument.

Below: A group of islanders at HMS *Raleigh*, the Royal Navy's training camp in Cornwall. The men were drafted in to serve aboard the navy's patrol vessels.

A group of soldiers of the 51st Highland Division Anti-Tank Regiment leaving from Millport pier in 1939.

Soldiers of 51st Highland Division Anti-Tank Regiment with their commander at Aldershot in 1940.

During the Second World War Garrison House was used as a hospital for convalescent soldiers. Here we see the Commandant, Lady Margaret MacRae, sister of the Marquis of Bute, with her team of nurses.

Members of the 6th Bute (Millport) Voluntary Aid Detachment making sheets in the Garrison grounds in preparation for the evacuated patients from a London hospital around 1940.

The Millport VADs that served during the Second World War. *From Left to right, back row:* Marie McLachlan; Molly Cameron; Jessie Hunter. *Middle row:* -?-; Jessie Dunn; Mrs Duncan; Isa Kidd; Mary Kerr; Eileen Turnbull; Jenny Kerr. *Front row:* Betty Kerr; Maggie Robertson; Jean Munro.

ARRIVAL OF COAL
MILLPORT 10/4/12

Ten

Maritime Millport

Everyone and everything that goes to the Cumbraes has to go by a boat of one description or other. The early vessels sailing in and out of the islands were small fishing smacks and cargo sloops, but perhaps the best remembered way of getting to Millport was aboard one of the famous Clyde pleasure steamers. These were sleek and graceful ships that criss-crossed the Clyde, taking commuters and holidaymakers to and from the islands. A trip on a steamer was a great social event and a fitting way to start and finish a memorable holiday. As a seaside resort, it was also inevitable that one of the pleasures of a holiday at Millport was playing about in rowing boats or yachts, both of which could be hired on the island.

All trade with the island also went by sea. Coal was one of the main cargoes to come to the island. It was not only needed for domestic fires but vast amounts were also needed to fuel Millport's gas supply. The advent of the 'roll-on roll-off' ferry service has changed the island's maritime traffic beyond all recognition. All cargo now comes by road and passengers have to get a bus into Millport from Cumbrae Slip. Only the occasional excursion boat now comes into Millport Pier.

Opposite: The arrival of the coal at Millport Pier on 10 April 1912 aboard the *Mary Kerr* and the *Jessie Kerr*.

The *Marchioness of Breadalbane* had a long association with the island and captured the hearts of Millport's residents and visitors. She was built in 1890 and soon afterwards was put on the Largs – Millport – Rothesay run. During the summer the ship was based at Millport and many locals were employed on the crew. She continued on this route until 1933 and, despite her age, she was held in high esteem.

A rather august body of Millport worthies, including ex-Provost John Taylor, enjoying a trip aboard the *Queen Alexandra* on the 15 September 1910.

A CLYDE SEAMAN'S SOLILOQUY

TO HIS SHIP,

S.S. "MARCHIONESS OF BREADALBANE."

You talk about the "Rothesay," the "Fife," and
    the "Argyll,"
And when I hear you talking, it often makes me
    smile;
For when the wind is howling, and the sea is
    running high,
You'll find the old "Breadalbane" when no other
    boat is nigh!

There, leaping o'er the billows, or diving to the
    mast,
She flies the Caley colours, all tattered with the
    blast;
She flies the Caley colours, so to her we'll give a
    cheer,
While the great and mighty steamers are moored at
    Rothesay pier.

So from Millport up to Rothesay, each day we're on
    the run,
And when we get a bleaching we take it all in fun;
For we know the old "Breadalbane" is as sturdy
    as a rock,
For we've seen her often tested with the fearful
    winter shock.

The travelling public know it, for they nearly break
    their necks
(And they don't forget to show it) when they rush
    upon her decks;
Though we tell them bigger steamers are bound for
    Rothesay Bay,
"Ah! we want the old 'Breadalbane,'" is all that
    they will say.

We have a good old skipper, and a mate, give them
    their due,
And as fine a lot of sailors, as ever formed a crew;
Our engineer and stokers can always make her hum,
If there's one to beat her record, from the stocks
    she'll have to come.

ARDRISHAIG.   WM. STEVENSON.

Among the archives of the museum in Millport is this rather fascinating handbill about the
Marchioness of Breadalbane which shows just how well loved she was.

P.S. *Marchioness of Lorne* was built in 1891 to sail between Ardrossan and Brodick but in fact spent several years on the Wemyss Bay to Millport summer service. Soon after she was built she was offered free of charge to the Millport Visitor's Club who ran a fund-raising evening cruise around the Isle of Bute with five hundred passengers aboard.

The crew of the *Marchioness of Lorne*.

Right: The 'ship's orchestra' entertaining passengers aboard the *Caledonia* in 1914. It was common for bands of musicians to travel aboard the Clyde steamers. Sometimes they were the official entertainment provided for the cruise but quite often they were simply busking to a captive audience hoping for a healthy whip-round.

Below: For thirteen years the *Talisman* was based at Millport during the summer season. She was built in 1935 as an experimental diesel electric paddle vessel. After a rather chequered career she was laid up waiting to be scrapped when she was given a reprieve and, in 1954, she was put on the Millport – Largs – Wemyss Bay run. She captured the hearts of the Cumbrae folk and was regarded as Millport's own paddle 'steamer'. Her crew entered into the spirit of Millport holiday life and *Talisman*'s football and tug of war teams regularly competed with the burgh and visitor's teams.

STEAMER AT PIER MILLPORT.

One of the great pleasures of a holiday in Millport was to hire a rowing boat and attempt a trip around the bay. Here we see a family, complete with their dog, valiantly setting forth from the stone jetty known as Strathwherry Pier on Newton Sands in 1913. Two families, the Mauchlines and the Hunters, controlled the boat hiring trade for many years and there was an intense rivalry between the two firms.

A view showing the boats along Strathwherry Pier. *The first thing a boy did on arrival was to gang up with the local boat hirers. I became a Mauchline boy, therefore being an arch enemy 'daggers drawn' with the Hunter clan. I was soon initiated into the seamanship of rowing boats. To become a good 'boy' meant being at the jetty early and taken out to a string of boats anchored in front of the Eileans and put aboard the first one. Under the board a tin was kept to bail out any water collected, the next boat pulled in and boarded, with the same procedure until the four boats were thus treated, then up anchor and a tow to the jetty where they were wiped clean with a rag and ready for customers. The price was 3d an hour. Each party was given the most suitable boat. When all members were seated the anchor was handed in and a push given to set them on their way.* From J.C.M.'s 'Millport Memories'.

The Mauchlines and Hunters also operated their own boat building yards to build the small dinghies and launches for their hiring trade. Alex Hunter operated the West Bay boatyard and James Mauchline owned a boatyard on Kames Street. Here we see the largest boat ever built on the island, James Mauchline's motor launch *Triumph III*, nearing completion in 1933.

The *Triumph III* taking a party of tourists on a trip in 1949. James Mauchline's motor boats, all called *Triumph*, made excursions to places such as Kilchattan Bay, Largs and Portencross and in the evenings would offer fishing trips with lines and bait supplied.

Some people's idea of a pleasure boat was a little different. Here we see *Erin*, the private yacht of Sir Thomas Lipton, presumably anchored in Millport Bay. Many of the great industrialists had their own steam yachts and as well as being used for their own pleasure they were also used to entertain and impress potential clients.

Fishing boats have operated from Cumbrae ever since the island was inhabited. Here we see some of the small Millport-based fishing boats in the harbour with a visiting Loch Fyne skiff from Greenock tied up alongside.

The *Mary Kerr* and *Jessie Kerr* served as Cumbrae's cargo boats over many years. They were owned by Walter Kerr and built in the 1880s by the Fife's of Fairlie boatyard. Among the cargoes that they carried were coal, sand, tiles and other building materials. The *Jessie Kerr* was lost at Ardrossan not long after this photograph was taken.

Walter Kerr's family continued the business and in 1926 the *Saxon* was purchased. This famous Clyde puffer served Millport for nearly forty years and was considered an integral part of the scenery of Millport Bay. Late in her career the *Saxon* featured as the *Vital Spark* in the original BBC series of Para Handy. Tied up alongside is the *Sunbeam*, one of Alex Hunter's motor launches.

Right: In 1844 two young seamen from the naval survey vessel HMS *Shearwater* were drowned off Tomont End on the north of the island. This monument was erected to their memory. The inscription, long since eroded, read: *To the memory of Mr Charles D. Cayley, aged 17 years and Mr William N. Jewall aged 19 years, Midshipmen of HMS Shearwater, promising young officers drowned in the upsetting of their boat near this place 17 May 1844. This monument is erected in token of their worth by Captain Robinson and officers of the above-named vessel.*

Opposite, above: The Cumbraes have seen their fair share of wrecks and maritime disasters. The *Lady Isabella* ran ashore close under the Cumbrae Lighthouse in December 1902. One local remembered the scene well: *The first that was known at Millport of the disaster was the following morning when one of the Clyde Shipping Company tugs with the crew on board came to Millport pier and the Lady Isabella's captain went to the post office, presumably to telegraph his company about her loss. Those of us who were on the pier learned from the ship's crew who were on the tug that one of them had swum ashore with a rope, made it fast to a rock, and so enabled the rest of the crew to make the shore. My brother John Murray and I boarded the Lady Isabella a few days later. She was then in a position much as shown in the photograph and close to under the lighthouse. I remember the thrill of going on board and of gazing aloft in wonder at the maze of rigging and ropes above.*

Opposite, below: An unfortunate accident occurred aboard the Irish schooner *Sarah Jane* on 13 March 1914. She had travelled over from Larne with a cargo of lime for local farmers. Whilst tied up at Millport pier she began taking on water. This reacted with the lime which then ignited. The three crewmen on board, Capt. McCalmont, William O'Neill and Edmond Montgomery, all died in the suffocating fumes. The boat was later towed out to the Eileans where she was completely destroyed by the fire.

The *Maid of Cumbrae* and the *Maid of Skelmorlie* at Millport pier in 1953. The 'maids' were built to replace the aging paddle steamer fleet on the Clyde. While they provided faithful service on the Largs to Millport run for over twenty years they failed to capture the affection that the paddlers had earned.

In 1965 a hovercraft service from Largs to Kames Bay was set up by Peter Kaye, an entrepreneur who lived on Little Cumbrae. He hoped that this would be the future for travel on the Clyde. The hovercraft was viewed with great excitement and it was affectionately nicknamed the 'skooshin cushion'. However, many people complained about the noise and apparently one lady who lived on the west side of Kames Bay complained about her ornaments vibrating on the mantelpiece as the hovercraft came in. Despite being popular with the tourists the venture proved uneconomic and the service only lasted for seven months. (Thanks to the Hovercraft Museum's website for this information.)

Cumbrae Slip opened in 1972 and for the first time allowed for a regular car ferry service from Largs. The first ferries were very small and could not cope with the volume of traffic. The *Isle of Cumbrae* was built in 1976 at Troon to cater for the increasing traffic that the service generated.

Regular sailings to Millport pier stopped in 1985 but excursion boats such as Clyde Marine Motoring's *Second Snark*, and of course the *Waverley*, continue to sail to Millport during the summer months.

LESSER CUMBRAE FROM MILLPORT.

Eleven

Wee Cumbrae

The island of Little, Lesser or Wee Cumbrae, as it is affectionately known, is of quite a different character to its larger neighbour. It is much more rugged and isolated and has been inhabited over the years by only a small number of people.

Among the early settlers was Saint Veya who established an early Christian settlement on the island in the seventh century. The remoteness of the island also made it attractive as a retreat for the early Scottish kings who used it as a safe haven. A number of crofter fishing families later settled on the island. In 1757 a beacon was erected on the top of the island to become the first navigation light on the Clyde and this was later replaced with a more modern lighthouse.

When Millport developed as a holiday resort in the mid-nineteenth century it became popular to have a day trip over to Wee Cumbrae and enjoy a ramble or a picnic. However, as the island was privately owned, access to the island was solely at the discretion of the owners. Changes in ownership of the island meant that it later became very difficult for casual visitors to enjoy the island. Current plans are to turn the island into an exclusive resort.

Opposite: Wee Cumbrae is seen here from the shores of Great Cumbrae.

Cumbrae Castle is thought to have been built by Walter, the steward who married Robert the Bruce's daughter Marjorie in 1315. Several charters of King Robert II were signed in the castle and it is thought that David II and Robert III also stayed in the castle. The island gradually fell out of favour with the Scottish monarchy and was inhabited by 'rebels, fugitives and excommunicates', not to mention 'disordered thieves'. In 1599 the castle was attacked by a band of thirty such men who broke down the doors, ousted the resident, and proceeded to live in the castle. The castle ceased to be a residence in 1653 when Cromwell's troops burnt the roof down.

In 1913 the island was purchased by Evelyn Parker for the sum of £5,000. The Parkers were a wealthy family and had a large house built close to the castle and laid out a garden that was designed by the famous garden designer Gertrude Jeckyll.

Wee Cumbrae was a popular destination for day trippers from Millport, both residents and visitors alike. Here we see Mrs Watt (holding the teapot) enjoying a picnic on the island with her friends and family in the 1930s.

In this late nineteenth century photograph we can see a couple of excursion boats lying in the bay.

The rugged nature of the island can be seen in this view of the lighthouse from the shore. The original coal fire beacon at the top of the island was soon found to be inadequate. It was highly inconvenient to drag all the coal up to the top of the island and even on a clear night the light was poor. The new lighthouse was built in a more suitable location but it was still a major operation to get all the necessary stores from the jetty up a hundred feet of cliff to the light.

Opposite, below: The lighthouse and the keepers' cottages were surrounded by a walled garden. This provided a welcome recreation for the lighthouse keepers and their families. No doubt it also helped to supplement their stores with fresh produce. The value of having this garden is shown by the fact that when the light was being extensively rebuilt in 1823 the keeper was granted £5 compensation 'for want of his garden'.

CUMBRAE LIGHTHOUSE SHOWING FIRST LIGHTHOUSE BUOY IN EXISTENCE

The new lighthouse was completed in 1793 and was built partly to the design of the esteemed Robert Stevenson who was then just nineteen years old. It was powered initially by whale oil and sent out a beam magnified by a series of mirrors. The Clyde Lighthouses Trust was the first to use flashing buoys as a navigational aid. The first of them was moored off Greenock in 1880. When the buoy was taken out of commission it was moved to the Cumbrae lighthouse for display.

CUMBRAE LIGHTHOUSE AND ARRAN HILLS, MILLPORT, ISLE OF CUMBRAE

127

MUSEUM OF
THE CUMBRAES

I thought it would be fitting to finish with this postcard which was specially created to celebrate the opening of the new Museum of the Cumbraes in Millport. The museum has a fascinating collection and provides an interesting insight into life on the island. It is well worth a visit.